GHASTLY GASES

WRITTEN BY MIKE CLARK

PowerKiDS press

Published in 2018 by
The Rosen Publishing Group, Inc.
29 East 21st Street, New York, NY 10010

Cataloging-in-Publication Data
Names: Clark, Mike.
Title: Ghastly gases / Mike Clark.
Description: New York : PowerKids Press, 2018. | Series: Strange
    science and explosive experiments | Includes index.
Identifiers: ISBN 9781538323649 (pbk.) | ISBN 9781538322680
    (library bound) | ISBN 9781538323656 (6 pack)
Subjects: LCSH: Change of state (Physics)--Experiments--Juvenile
    literature. | Science--Experiments--Juvenile literature.
Classification: LCC QC301.C53 2018 | DDC 530.078--dc23

Written by: Mike Clark
Edited by: Charlie Ogden
Designed by: Matt Rumbelow

Photoc redits: Abbreviations: l-left, r-right, b-bottom, t-top, c-center, m-middle. All images
courtesy of Shutterstock, unless otherwise specified. With thanks to 2 – curraheeshutter. 4: tr
– Tim UR; m – CAN BALCIOGLU. 5 – paulista. 6 – Polryaz. 7 – Pro_Stock. 8: tl – Yellow Cat; bl –
Evlakhov Valeriy; r – givaga. 10: tr – onthewaybackhome; m – Roman Sigaev; bl – Aleksandr
Pobedimskiy; bm – Valentyn Volkov. 11: Gus Pasquarella / wikipedia. 12 – Jaroslav Monchak.
13 – Taras Kushnir. 14: tr – Dmitry Kolmakov; tl – Zovteva; bl – Evgeny Karandaev; bc – Africa
Studio; mr – Gts; br – timquo. 15: tr – O.Bellini; mr – wk1003mike; 16: bl – Jacek Chabraszewski;
br – Ramon Espelt Photography. 17 – Jess Wealleans. 18: l – Kerdkanno; Mr – happymay; br
– Photosiber. 19: tr – ajt; ml – Africa Studio; 19 br – WaiveFamisoCZ. 20: bg – T. L. Furrer; bl
– Juan Gaertner. 21 – Nils Z. 22 – Kekyalyaynen. 23 – Damir Sencar. 24 – igorstevanovic. 25
– TfoxFoto. 27: bg – Archiwiz; Front – kevin brine. 28: tr – Everett Historical; bl – Polarpx; br –
Photographisches Institut der ETH Zürich / wikipedia. 29: l – MIA Studio; b – Meryll.

Manufactured in China
CPSIA Compliance Information: Batch BW18PK: For Further Information contact
Rosen Publishing, New York, New York at 1-800-237-9932.

CONTENTS

Page 4   **Grasping Gas**

Page 6   **Volatile Volume**

Page 8   **Bloating Balloons**

Page 10   **Extreme Evaporation**

Page 12   **Almighty Atmosphere**

Page 14   **Balloon Blast**

Page 16   **Stinky Smells**

Page 18   **Tricky Tasting**

Page 20   **Foul Flatulence**

Page 22   **Pollution Peril**

Page 24   **Goofy Gas Masks**

Page 26   **Crafty Chemists**

Page 30   **Quick Quiz**

Page 31   **Glossary**

Page 32   **Index**

Words that appear like **this** can be found in the glossary on page 31.

Grasping Gas

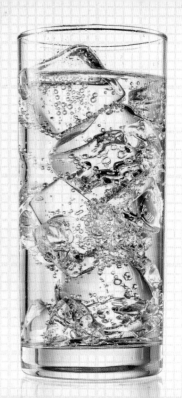

Gas makes up the air we breathe and is one of the three main states of matter. Matter is anything that has weight and volume, such as water. The three main states of matter are solid, liquid, and gas. Water can exist in all states of matter. When water is a solid it's called ice, when it's a liquid it's called water, and when it's a gas it's called water vapor or steam.

When water is boiled, it turns into steam. Steam takes up more space than water. This is because when water is boiled, the **atoms** of the water move away from each other and fill more space. Steam – along with other gases – is harder to see than a liquid because all the atoms are more spread out.

Matter is also lighter when it is a gas than when it is a liquid. This is because when the atoms are spread out, fewer atoms can fit in a certain amount of space. For example, a glass of steam would weigh less than a glass of water. A glass of ice would also weigh less than a glass of water because, unlike liquids, solids cannot expand freely to fill the space.

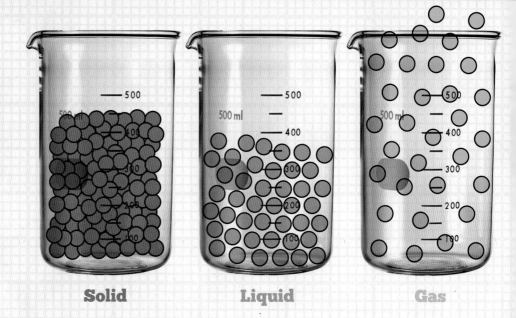

Solid   **Liquid**   **Gas**

ATOMS ARE SO SMALL THAT A SINGLE DROP OF WATER WILL HAVE OVER 1,000,000,000,000,000,000,000 ATOMS.

Volatile Volume

When atoms are spaced apart, they take up more space. The amount of space that matter takes up is called volume. When matter is a gas, the atoms are spaced far apart and they take up more space. This is why gas always has a greater volume than the other states of matter — liquid and solid. The atoms in solids and liquids are closer together.

Gases, like steam, are formed when a liquid is heated. For example, when a kettle is turned on, the atoms in the water are heated up. The heat then causes the atoms to move around and become spaced apart. When the atoms in the water get hot enough, they will be moving so fast that they will move away from each other and float off into the air as steam.

If you capture the steam and cool it, this will slow the atoms down. This means the atoms will move closer together and become a liquid again. You can do this by carefully holding something cold over a steaming cup of water. The water will **condense** on the cold object because the cold object will cool the atoms that make up the water.

STEAM CONDENSES BACK TO WATER WHEN IT HITS COLD GLASS.

Bloating Balloons

Lots of gases make up the air we breathe. Most of the air is made up of the gases nitrogen and oxygen, but there is also a small amount of a gas called carbon dioxide. It would take extremely cold temperatures to make the atoms in these gases come together close enough to form a liquid. However, even if these gases are only slightly cooled, they will still shrink because their atoms will come closer together. You can see this shrinking effect with an easy experiment. All you will need is:

BOWL

BALLOON

BOTTLE OF SODA

Step 1)

Blow up the balloon a little but not all the way. Unscrew the cap off the soda bottle and place the opening of the balloon around the opening of the soda bottle.

Step 2)

Place the balloon and bottle into a freezer and leave it for about ten minutes.

Step 3)

After ten minutes, fill up a bowl with warm water. Now remove the bottle and balloon from the freezer. Notice that the balloon has gone down. Submerge the bottle in the warm water and watch the balloon inflate again.

The balloon shrank at first because the atoms that make up the air in the bottle and balloon became cooler. When the atoms became cooler, they slowed down and moved around less. As they moved around less, they moved closer together. This results in the air taking up less space. When they were warmed up, they moved around more again and took up more space.

HOT AIR IS LIGHTER THAN COLD AIR BECAUSE THE ATOMS ARE FARTHER APART. THIS IS HOW HOT AIR BALLOONS FLOAT.

Extreme Evaporation

All matter turns into a gas when heated. This is called evaporation. However, it will take a higher temperature to turn some types of matter into gas than other types of matter. For example, a metal such as iron would need to be heated to about 5,432°F (3,000°C) before it would turn into a gas. Water, on the other hand, only needs to be heated to 212°F (100°C).

ICE (SOLID WATER)

IRON

Some atoms need higher temperatures than others to turn into a gas. This is because some atoms are heavier than others. Heavier atoms need more heat before they can move away from each other. Iron has atoms that are much heavier than the atoms in water. This is why iron needs more heat to turn into a gas.

IN 1937, A ZEPPELIN CAUGHT FIRE AND EXPLODED BECAUSE IT USED HYDROGEN.

Some gases are made of very light atoms, so light that they can even be used to make objects float. For example, helium is a gas that has atoms so light that it can be used to make balloons float.

Another gas with very light atoms is called hydrogen. It was once used in **airships,** but hydrogen is very **flammable**. This is why airships now use helium instead.

Almighty Atmosphere

Most of the gases on Earth are floating around in the air that we breathe. This air makes up our atmosphere, which is the layer of gases that surround the globe. The atmosphere is made mostly of two gases — nitrogen and oxygen.

The air pushes down on everything on the ground. It pushes on us from every direction. This weight pressing down on us is known as atmospheric pressure because it is coming from the Earth's atmosphere. The atmospheric pressure is greatest at **sea level**. This is because, at sea level, more air is pushing down on you from above. Atmospheric pressure is weakest at the top of mountains because there is less air pushing down on you from above.

Atmospheric Pressure

The atoms in the air at the top of mountains are very far apart because there is less pressure pushing them close together. This means there are smaller amounts of oxygen in the air at the top of mountains. Mountain climbers often experience a type of sickness called altitude sickness when they climb to the top of mountains. This is because the lack of oxygen can cause their bodies to feel sick and dizzy.

Balloon Blast

Air pressure is a powerful force. When gas that is under high pressure is released into gas that is under low pressure, the results can be very dramatic. To see air pressure at work all you need is:

FUNNEL

TABLESPOON

BAKING SODA

Household Uses
Fresh Box

Net WT 17.5 OZ (500gr)

VINEGAR　　**PLASTIC BOTTLE**

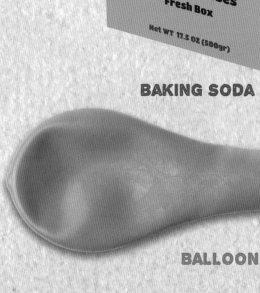

BALLOON

Step 1)

Fill your empty bottle with two tablespoons of vinegar.

Step 2)

Using a funnel, fill your deflated balloon with two tablespoons of baking soda. Pinch the neck of your balloon so the baking soda doesn't fall out, then attach it to the neck of your bottle.

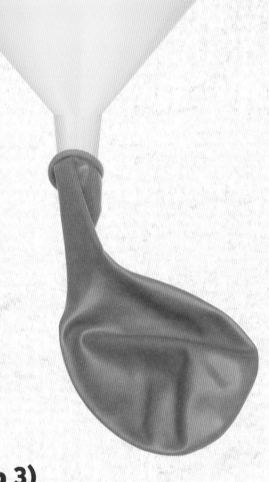

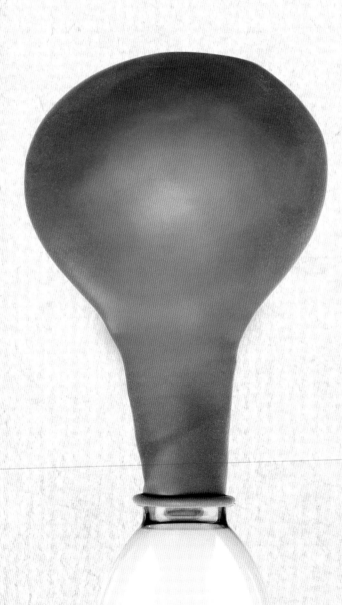

Step 3)

Let go of the balloon's neck and hold it upright, allowing the baking powder to fall into the bottle. Now give it a good shake!

The mixture of baking soda and vinegar creates carbon dioxide. The buildup of this new gas means the air pressure in the bottle increases. This air needs to go somewhere so it will begin to fill the balloon and cause it to inflate.

Stinky Smells

Gas is very important for our sense of smell. When our dinner is hot, it creates steam. As steam rises, it carries some particles of our food with it. These particles enter our nose and hit a special smell sensing area called the olfactory epithelium. Information is then sent to the brain about how the food smells.

Food that smells bad is sensed in exactly the same way, but the gases are not coming from steam. The horrible smell of spoiled milk, rotten eggs, or moldy fruit is carried in gases coming from fungi and bacteria, which are **microscopic** creatures. When bacteria eat our food, they release a foul-smelling gas that our noses can detect. By picking up on this bad smell, our bodies are keeping us safe from bacteria that could make us sick.

DOGS CAN SMELL UP TO 40 TIMES BETTER THAN HUMANS, BECAUSE THEIR OLFACTORY EPITHELIUM IS LARGER.

Tricky Tasting

Our sense of smell is very important to our sense of taste. If we smell something else while we are eating, it can change how our food tastes. You can experiment with this effect easily. All you need is:

A RANGE OF TASTY FOOD

A RANGE OF NOT SO TASTY FOOD

Step 1)

Close your eyes and have a friend give you a piece of food to hold under your nose.

Step 2)

Now have your friend give you a different piece of food for you to eat while you continue to smell the first piece of food.

Step 3)

Try several different combinations. You should find that the taste of the food was very different than normal, or it might have been impossible to tell which food you were eating.

The reason the food tastes different is because your brain is mixing two types of information together. It is mixing the smell from your nose and the flavor from the taste buds on your tongue. This creates a weird taste in your mouth.

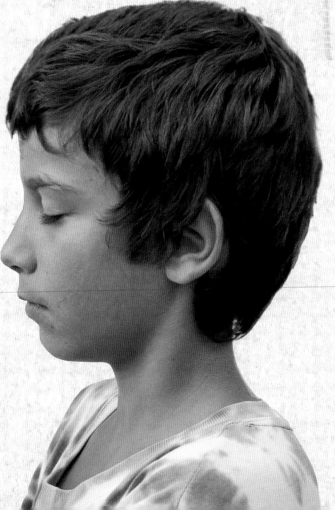

Foul Flatulence

Flatulence, or "passing wind," is one ghastly gas that we all make! The human body makes about 17 ounces (0.5 l) every day, but the gas isn't actually made by us. The gas that we pass is actually made by a group of bacteria in our gut called the gut flora. The gut flora produce gas when they munch on the food in your gut.

The foulness of your flatulence depends on what types of bacteria live in your gut, but also on what you eat. Certain foods are harder to break down than others. Your gut is filled with **enzymes** that break down food, but they cannot always break down everything. The food that gets left over is eaten by your gut flora.

Beans often get the blame for foul flatulence. This is because they are high in fiber, which is hard for the body's enzymes to break down. As a result, plenty will be left over for the bacteria to eat, which will create a lot of gas!

Pollution Peril

Pollution is the introduction of harmful substances that can cause damage to the **environment**. Pollution from harmful gases is one of the worst forms of pollution because it is very difficult to clean up gas once it has been released. A pollutant is a substance that can cause damage to the environment. One of the biggest pollutants is the gas we call carbon dioxide.

Carbon dioxide is a very common gas. When animals, including ourselves, breathe in oxygen, we breathe out carbon dioxide as waste. However, this carbon dioxide is then used by plants, which give out oxygen as their waste. This creates a balance between plants and animals.

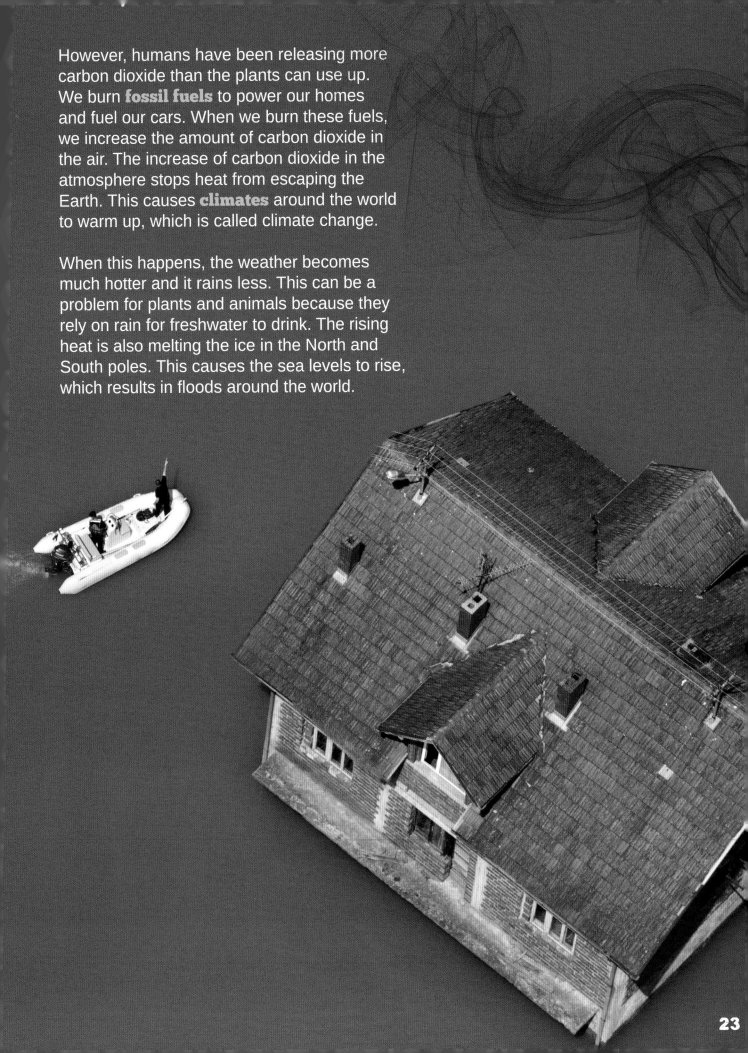

However, humans have been releasing more carbon dioxide than the plants can use up. We burn **fossil fuels** to power our homes and fuel our cars. When we burn these fuels, we increase the amount of carbon dioxide in the air. The increase of carbon dioxide in the atmosphere stops heat from escaping the Earth. This causes **climates** around the world to warm up, which is called climate change.

When this happens, the weather becomes much hotter and it rains less. This can be a problem for plants and animals because they rely on rain for freshwater to drink. The rising heat is also melting the ice in the North and South poles. This causes the sea levels to rise, which results in floods around the world.

Goofy Gas Masks

Gas masks were made during World War I, when deadly gases were used to kill soldiers. The gas mask was designed to stop soldiers breathing in dangerous gas from the air. By breathing air through the filter of the gas mask, the deadly atoms of gas were removed.

The gas mask works because the atoms of deadly gases are larger than oxygen atoms. Gas mask filters trap the large, deadly atoms, but let the small oxygen atoms pass straight through. Therefore, the person wearing the mask does not breathe in any deadly gas.

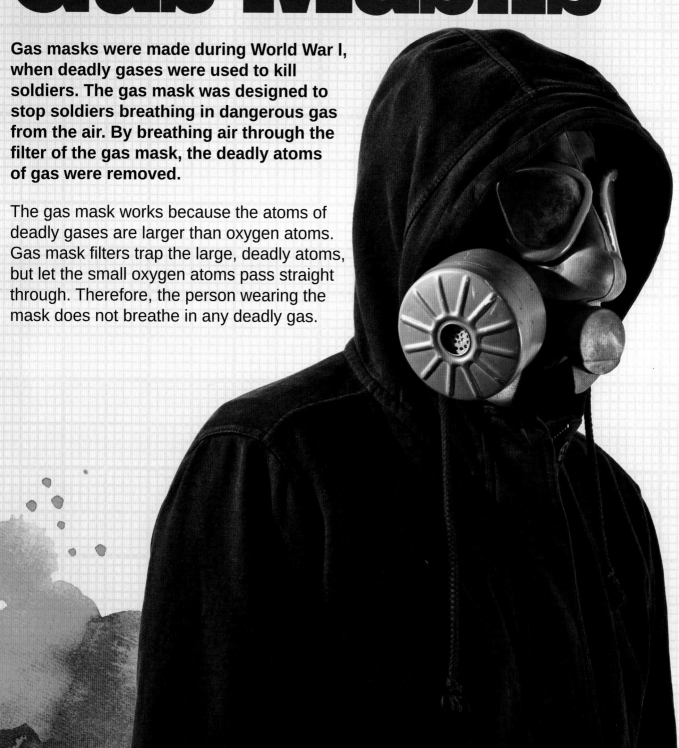

However, gas masks are only useful if there is enough oxygen in the air to breathe. Wearing a gas mask in a raging fire would be useless. When a fire burns materials, it uses up oxygen in the air while also releasing a lot of deadly gases at the same time. This is why firefighters have to wear oxygen masks. Oxygen masks don't clean the existing air, but instead provide clean air from a tank strapped to the firefighter's back.

Crafty Chemists

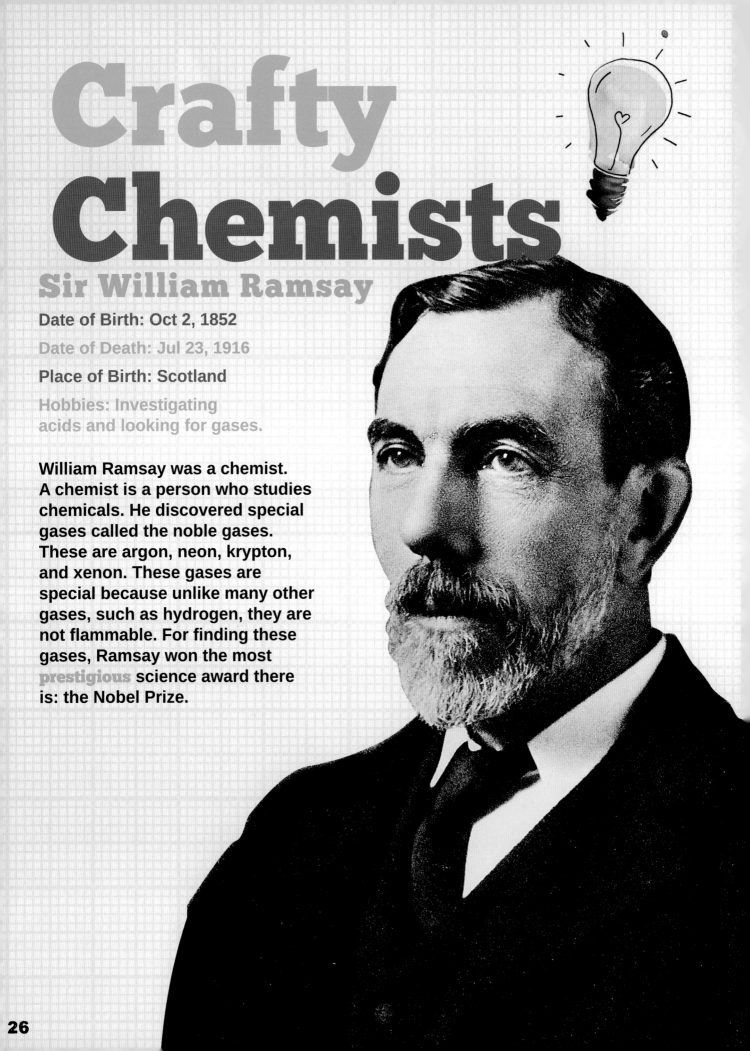

Sir William Ramsay

Date of Birth: Oct 2, 1852

Date of Death: Jul 23, 1916

Place of Birth: Scotland

Hobbies: Investigating acids and looking for gases.

William Ramsay was a chemist. A chemist is a person who studies chemicals. He discovered special gases called the noble gases. These are argon, neon, krypton, and xenon. These gases are special because unlike many other gases, such as hydrogen, they are not flammable. For finding these gases, Ramsay won the most prestigious science award there is: the Nobel Prize.

Ramsay also figured out how to separate helium. At the time, this gas was hard to find. Because helium is so light, natural sources of the gas would float away and be lost. Ramsay knew that helium needed to be made where it could be easily captured.

Four of the gases, argon, neon, krypton, and xenon, are often used in electric lights. Argon is used in light bulbs. Neon glows when electricity is passed through it, so it is placed into long tubes to create lights that can be bent into fun shapes. Krypton and xenon glow extremely bright when electricity is passed through them, which is why they are used for lighthouses.

Fritz Haber

Date of Birth: Dec 9, 1868

Date of Death: Jan 29, 1934

Place of Birth: Prussia (Poland)

Hobbies: Discovering how to save lives, then discovering how to kill people.

Fritz Haber was a chemist whose discoveries were both lifesaving and life destroying. In 1918, he won the Nobel Prize for discovering how to produce ammonia. Ammonia is a gas which can be used on fields to grow crops. This discovery saved thousands from the threat of starvation and famine.

However, during World War I, Haber made a much more destructive discovery. He figured out how to make and use a very dangerous gas called chlorine in weapons. These weapons were then used to kill thousands of soldiers.

Ammonia is a very important gas for plants, and they cannot grow without it. Ammonia is naturally found in animal urine (pee) and feces (poo). This gets into the soil and helps plants to grow. However, farmers were growing and gathering crops so quickly that the ammonia in the soil could not be replaced by the animals fast enough. If this continued, many people would have starved. However, thanks to Haber, we can now make as much ammonia as we want. Now farmers can just pour it over their land. This means we can grow more food.

THE AMMONIA MADE USING HABER'S METHOD DOESN'T COME FROM PEE OR POO. IT IS MADE BY HEATING AND COOLING NITROGEN AND HYDROGEN GASES.

QUICK QUIZ

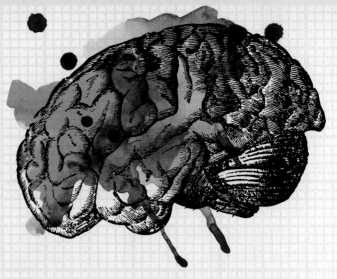

HAVE YOU TAKEN IT ALL IN? TAKE THIS QUICK QUIZ TO TEST YOUR KNOWLEDGE. THE ANSWERS ARE UPSIDE DOWN AT THE BOTTOM OF THE PAGE.

1. What are the three states of matter?

2. What happens to the atoms in boiling water?

3. At what temperature does water turn into steam?

4. Where is atmospheric pressure greatest?

5. What is the name of the area in your nose that senses smells?

6. What is the name for the microscopic creatures in our gut that cause flatulence?

7. What gas is released when we burn fossil fuels that causes climate change?

8. What is the name of the gas that a gas mask allows through its filter?

9. What can neon gas be used for?

10. What gas did Fritz Haber figure out how to make that saved many lives from starvation?

1) Solid, Liquid, and Gas 2) They move away from each other 3) 212°F (100°C) 4) At sea level 5) Olfactory epithelium 6) Gut flora 7) Carbon dioxide 8) Oxygen 9) Lights 10) Ammonia

GLOSSARY

airships   a type of aircraft that is kept afloat by a body of gas

atoms   tiny particles that all matter is made up of

climates   the common weather conditions in certain places

condense   change from a gas or vapor into a liquid

crops   plants that are grown on a large scale because they are useful, usually as food

environment   the natural world

enzymes   substances made by living things that help the body in lots of ways, such as by breaking down food

flammable   easily ignited and burnt

fossil fuels   fuels such as coal, oil, and gas, that formed millions of years ago from the remains of animals and plants

microscopic   so small it can only be viewed under a microscope

prestigious   having a high status that is respected and admired

sea level   the level of the sea's surface

starvation   suffering or death caused by lack of food

INDEX

air 4, 6, 8-9, 12-13, 15, 23, 24-25

air pressure 14-15, 23

airships 11

atmosphere 12, 23

atmospheric pressure 12, 13, 30

atoms 4-11, 13, 24, 30

bacteria 16, 20-21

balloons 8-9, 11, 14-15

breathing 4, 8, 12, 22, 24-25

carbon dioxide 8, 15, 22-23, 30

climate change 23, 30

condensation 7

cooling 7-9, 29

evaporation 10

fire 11, 25

flatulence 20-21, 30

freezing 9

gas masks 24-25, 30

Haber, Fritz 28-29, 30

helium 11, 27

hydrogen 11, 26, 29

ice 4, 10, 23

iron 10

matter 4, 6, 10, 30

nitrogen 8, 12, 29

oxygen 8, 12-13, 22, 24-25, 30

pollution 22

pressure 12-15, 30

Ramsay, William 26-27

smelling 16-19, 30

steam 4, 6-7, 16

tasting 18-19

volume 4, 6

water 4-7, 9-10, 23, 30